STRENGTH *of* SPIRIT

by Halima Hadavi

PEARSON

Glenview, Illinois • Boston, Massachusetts • Chandler, Arizona
Upper Saddle River, New Jersey

Helen Keller   Franklin D. Roosevelt

Many people have problems with their bodies. Some people cannot see or hear. Others cannot walk. We call these problems disabilities.

Helen Keller and Franklin D. Roosevelt both had disabilities. They also had much success. They even became friends.

Helen Keller
(1880–1968)

Helen Keller was born in Alabama. When she was two, she got sick. She became deaf. She could not hear. She also became blind. She could not see.

As she grew up, Helen was angry. She screamed. She broke things. Her parents did not know what to do.

Annie helped Helen learn words.

Helen's parents got a teacher for her. Her name was Annie Sullivan.

Annie taught Helen words. She spelled words into Helen's hand. Annie spelled C-A-K-E. Then she gave Helen a piece of cake.

At first, Helen did not understand. She did not know Annie was spelling words.

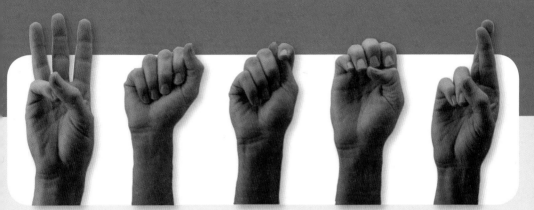

These finger shapes spell the word *water* in Sign Language.

After one month, something happened. Helen touched water. Annie spelled W-A-T-E-R in Helen's other hand. She spelled it again and again.

Helen understood! She was very excited. She began to touch everything. Annie spelled the name of each thing.

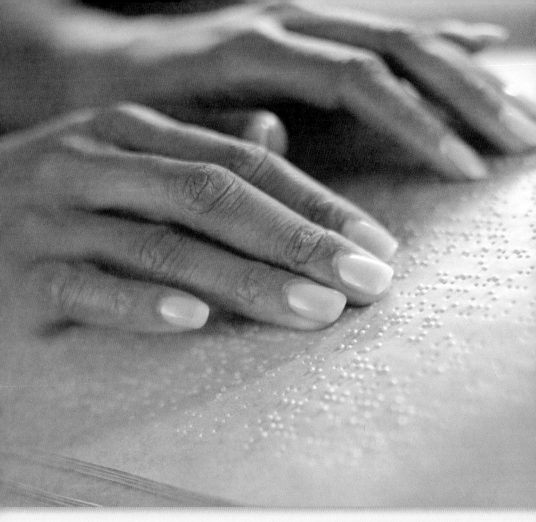

Blind people use Braille dots to read.

After that, Helen learned quickly. She studied math. She read stories in Braille. Braille is a way for people who are blind to read. They feel dots on a page. The dots stand for letters and words.

Helen Keller and Annie Sullivan

At age 20, Helen went to college. Annie went with her. She helped Helen study. She helped Helen write a book about her life.

Later, Helen and Annie went to many places. Helen told people about her life. Annie spoke Helen's words for her.

Helen wrote more books. She was even in movies about her life.

Helen Keller with
President Calvin
Coolidge in 1926

Helen helped blind and deaf people all over the
world. At this time, many people who were blind did
not get an education. Helen wanted this to change. She
raised money for a group that helped blind people.

Helen met many people. She met President Franklin
Roosevelt. He also had a disability.

Franklin Delano Roosevelt
(1882–1945)

Franklin Delano Roosevelt was born in New York. He went to college. Then he became a politician. His life was good. Then in 1921, everything changed.

Roosevelt got very sick. At first, his legs hurt. He felt hot. Next, he could not feel his back. Then he could not feel his arms and legs.

The doctors told Roosevelt that he had polio. Polio is a disease. People with polio cannot move parts of their bodies. At age 39, Roosevelt would never walk again.

Franklin Roosevelt talked on the radio. He gave hope to millions of people.

Roosevelt wanted to help other people with disabilities. He bought land in Georgia. People with disabilities went there for help.

In 1933, Roosevelt became President of the United States. At that time, people were poor and hungry. Roosevelt helped them. He gave people jobs and hope. During World War II, Roosevelt was a strong leader.

People still read Helen Keller's books today.

Roosevelt's picture was put on a dime in 1946.

Roosevelt wanted a cure for polio. He raised money. He asked each American to send one dime. Soon the White House was full of dimes.

By 1955, a vaccine for polio was made. A vaccine is a medicine that keeps people safe from a disease.

Great Success

Helen Keller and Franklin D. Roosevelt both had disabilities. Yet they both had great success. They made people's lives better. Their hard work made a difference!